On being happy

By Patrick Yee

CHRONICLE BOOKS

SAN FRANCISCO

ISBN: 0-8118-0496-8

Jacket Design: Anne Shannon
Jacket Illustrations: Patrick Yee
Hand Lettering: Georgia Deaver

Printed in Hong Kong.
Library of Congress Cataloging-in-
Publication Data available.

Distributed in Canada by Raincoast Books
8680 Cambie Street
Vancouver, B.C. V6P 6M9

10 9 8 7 6 5 4 3 2

Chronicle Books
275 Fifth Street
San Francisco, California 94103

On being happy

spring dawn

lambs

good morning

calm lake

long walks

picnics

butterflies

raindrops

daisies

starry night

summertime

sunny day

at the beach

seagulls

hello dog

ocean breeze

lighthouse

harbor lights

bon voyage

sweet dreams

sunday morning

quiet place

windy day

beautiful song

open space

harvest time

sunset

brightly colored leaves

first snow

cold morning

snowflakes

friends

time alone

leading home

cooking supper

warm fires

night sky

wish you were here